The Most Important Minute

In Your Network Marketing Career

KEN DUNN

ISBN 978-0-9868368-0-0

Published by EvolvLife Publishing, a wholly owned subsidiary of EvolvLife Team Inc.

1305 Morningside Drive, Unit 15
Scarborough, Ontario, Canada L1N2S8
Phone: 1 (416) 477-1219

www.evolvlifepublishing.com
www.kendunnleadership.com
www.nextcenturywealth.com

Printed in Canada

Dedication

To Julie, my amazing best friend and wife. I can never repay you for your support, patience, trust, love and respect. You have been my rock through our own amazing race. Thank you for your help editing this book and editing my life!

To Matthew and Laura. I am so proud of both of you. You make me laugh and cry. You make me so happy to be a dad.

To my best friends in the entire world, Juan Carlos and Hortensia Barrios, thank you so much for teaching me, loving me, and encouraging me. You are an amazing example of leadership in today's world.

A special thanks to Trey White and Brent Hicks for refusing to play inside the box and trusting my friends and I with your dreams.

To Orjan and Hilde Saele for welcoming Julie and me into your lives and trusting me with your family.

To Art and Ann Jonak. I can never repay you for trusting me and broadening my perspective on this incredible profession. I will always be at your beck and call. We love you.

To Orrin Woodward, Randy Gage, Donna Johnson, Jordan Adler, Tom "Big Al" Schreiter, Richard Brook, Michael Clouse, Donna Imson and the many others that have taught me, motivated me, and inspired me. Thank you!

To Mike and Stacy Healy, Rod and Amy Emory, James and Casey Wood, Leonardo and Lilan Daniel, Luis and Milagro Allemant, Esperanza Birreuta, Angel and Justice Nieves, Joseph and Anna Berliarang, and the millions of others who believe.

Thank you!

Contents

Introduction

What if your entire network marketing career, your success or failure, the speed at which your business becomes profitable, the rate at which your business grows, even your retention in your business, could be narrowed down to one minute? Would you be interested in knowing what that one minute was? If you knew exactly when that precious moment in time was, would you be interested in knowing how to best use it?

During my career in network marketing, I have been very blessed. I have had the chance to get to know thousands of people who I call friends. I have traveled all over the world, and I have had hundreds of thousands of people join me in the business. After helping over 400 people personally get started in the business, I realized that an independent associate's chances of being successful are increased one hundred fold by their understanding of The Most Important Minute and how to use it properly.

I started writing this book from seat 6E on American Airlines flight 1409 to San Juan, Puerto Rico on December 6, 2010. I was heading down to paradise to work with some amazing network marketing professionals for a couple of days. Over the past several years, I have had the pleasure of speaking to more people than I can recall about success in network marketing. The more time I spend talking about getting started, developing your why, setting goals, mindset, prospecting, and the many other crucial subjects in our business, the more I realized that by understanding, and properly using, the most important minute in your career properly, it will increase the likelihood that you are going to have a positive experience.

I have intentionally written this book in a completely generic fashion so that you can apply The Most Important Minute strategies to whatever business you have chosen. Many of my friends have already started to buy large quantities of the book to give to their teams. I am sure that you will find the information and strategies valuable enough that you will want to do the same thing.

Once you learn how to use these properly, you will easily be able to teach it to your team. I have taught network marketing professionals around the world how to identify and use The Most Important Minute properly, and realize that these strategies work in any culture or country, in any company, and with any product or service.

We all know that when you start your network marketing business there are many skills you will have to learn if you are going to be successful. We will look at these skills and review some of the basics of the business. We will also identify The Most Important Minute together and then prove that using the strategies properly will save years of pain and anxiety.

Before we get into subject of our book, let's take some time to understand that there really are three phases someone will go through in his or her network marketing career. It has taken me years to understand this. In Malcolm Gladwell's book Outliers, he talks about the common traits possessed by the world's super producers. One of the main points of the book was that all of the world's greatest leaders had amassed 10,000 hours of experience in their chosen field. As I collected my 10,000 hours, it became extremely clear to me that there really are three phases that we go through as we build the business. I heard it once expressed like this: We have to bring them in, keep them in, and move them along. Identifying The Most Important Minute starts with understanding that there really are three types of people, or three phases that you will go through in our business and this book will show you how to bring them in, keep them in, and move them along.

Section 1: Bring Them In!

Chapter 1: The Prospect, the Apprentice, and the Mentor

"Leadership is influence."
John C. Maxwell

If we are going to really identify and learn to use The Most Important Minute properly then we should first understand the three phases of a network marketing professional's career. Understanding the differences between a prospect, an apprentice, and a mentor are crucial. Also, we need to realize that you cannot put the cart before the horse, as they say. You will find making money easier after you decide to become a better leader; you cannot become a better leader until you become a mentor; you cannot become a mentor until you become an apprentice; and you cannot become an apprentice unless you have been a prospect.

The prospect

(Merriam-Webster's, 2010 noun _prä-_spekt\\ Definition of PROSPECT 1a: a potential buyer or customer b: a likely candidate for a job or a position)

Before I joined the profession, I was a police detective. I spent fourteen years of my life investigating everything from drug trafficking, child abuse, white-collar crime, aggravated sexual assaults, weapons trafficking, and homicides. I was introduced to network marketing when I was 32. At the time, I had already decided I wanted to get out of policing. My wife Julie had just given birth to our second baby, a beautiful little girl we named Laura Jewel. Matthew, Laura's brother, was already two years old. It was when Matthew was born that I decided I needed to get out of policing. By then I was twelve years into the career, and I was in debt over my head.

Two years earlier I started a couple of home businesses in an effort to bring in some extra money. It took me a couple of years, about 2000 hours, and approximately 100 personally sponsored partners to realize my story was not that special. In fact, over 90 percent of people who join our profession are doing so for the same reasons.

The reality today is that most people are carrying more debt than ever. There are statistics in many countries that show that people are actually bringing home less after tax dollars today than three decades ago. The biggest reasons for less after-tax dollars is that our governments are constantly raising taxes in order to create extra money to fund ideas and solutions aimed at reducing poverty, and giving us a better standard of living. What an oxymoron! Here's a thought: lower taxes, give us back our money, and let us figure it out.

The reality is that the vast majority of people who are taking on network marketing as a profession are doing so because they are sick and tired of being sick and tired. There are some exceptions to the rule, but the best prospects are folks like you and me. Here is a good list of criteria for your average prospect joining a network marketing business:

Age:	30+
Gender:	60 percent women
Marital status:	The profession attracts both married and single people.
Family status:	1+ children
Employment status:	Varied, however the vast majority are employees, small business owners, and stay-at-home parents.
Financial Status:	Paycheck to paycheck with minimal savings

In my last book, *Being the Change* (EvolvLife Publishing in 2011), you can learn lots of incredible information about how I find these prospects and convert them into business-building partners.

By the time I sponsored 200 people in the business, I realized the reasons people were joining the business were so varied that it was hard to track. The only thing I can find in common with all the people I have sponsored is that they are all joining me. Prospects all want to make more money, want more free time, want better lives for their families, and a myriad of other reasons. The main reason some people sponsor at will, while others struggle for their first partner, is the reason you see in the mirror.

After we uncover *The Most Important Minute* in your career, we will take a look at the importance of leadership development in the prospecting process. The reality is people will not join your business unless they like you. You could have the greatest product, service, and opportunity on the planet, but if they don't like you, they will not join. In your network marketing career, you need to make the decision to become a better leader. If you are considering joining a network marketing business, then you are a prospect. Make sure to take the time to get to know the people you are going to be working with, and that you really do like them.

The apprentice

(Merriam-Webster's, 2010: noun, often attributive _-pren-t_s\ APPRENTICE
1a: one bound by indenture to serve another for a prescribed period with a view to learning an art or trade b: one who is learning by practical experience under skilled workers a trade, art, or calling 2: an inexperienced person: novice <an apprentice in cooking>)

When a prospect joins the business with you, they become your apprentice. If you just joined your network marketing company, then you are the apprentice. I love the term apprentice because it describes perfectly the mental state of the person who joins the business, and it sets the mindset for the sponsor. Think about when a student gets his certificate/degree as an automobile mechanic, or an engineer, or a doctor, or a lawyer. The student is simultaneously excited and scared. Excited because the classroom education is done and now they can start paying off those student loans, and scared because they are on their own. Now think about those first couple of months as an apprentice. The apprentice is monitored closely, given enough room to work and to move forward, but under the watchful eye of a journeyman who has clocked the 10,000 hours, been around the block, and got the T-shirt.

If you have just joined the team then you are an apprentice.

When I joined my first network marketing business, I was an apprentice. I wish someone had told me that! The biggest mistake someone can make when they join the business is to think that because of some unrelated success in life, or simple arrogance, that they can figure this out on their own. These people seldom ever succeed, and if they do, it takes longer and is more painful. If you are an apprentice right now, or are deciding to start over again and become an apprentice, grab a highlighter and start making notes in this book. Learning about the most important minute and how to use it will save you years of pain.

As an apprentice, you may need to reach out into your team for a mentor. In a perfect world, a responsible sponsor would have introduced you to the business. Sadly, that is seldom the case. If you were sponsored by someone who cares about you and is following the principles in this book then thank God right now! If you are realizing that you are on your own, don't worry as this book and the associated learning materials will serve as your adopted sponsor. The reality of my own experience in this business is that it was when I started to read the right books and listen to the right CDs that my business truly exploded. Either way, get ready to start learning and start growing. You won't grow your business until you start growing yourself!

The big difference between an apprentice in NWM & in other scenarios is that in our profession you don't have to wait to graduate or get a certificate. As soon as possible graduate yourself. The sooner you become independent the better. You need to be the leader of your team.

The mentor

(**Merriam-Webster's, 2010 1men·tor noun _men-_t_r, -t_r**
Definition of MENTOR
1: a friend of Odysseus entrusted with the education of Odysseus' son Telemachus 2a: a trusted counselor or guide b: tutor, coach)

In later chapters of the book you are going to learn some great techniques to get your business started properly, like what you should do in the first days, weeks, and months. You will also be given step-by-step instruction to make your business profitable in the short term. As you make money, you will realize that leadership is determined by the actions you take when no one is looking.

As you start to build a team and decide to be a responsible sponsor, you will spend time getting other people started. Your income in the business will be directly related to the example you set for other people, and to how many people you help get started properly. As your business grows, you should be spending more and more time working in the depths of your business. That means you will work one-on-one with people who are ten, twenty, even hundreds of levels deep in your organization.

I spent my entire adult life in investigative policing, and was fully equipped with a dominant, dictator-like personality. From the day I started the business, I had no problem signing up people, but I had no idea how to get people started properly and to create duplication. I really should apologize to the first hundred people I signed up as I had no idea what I was doing, and would do it all differently if I could start over. The attrition (drop out) rate in my first two years was terrible.

As a leader, it is crucial you get your personally sponsored people started properly. It is the only way to create duplication in your group. As children, we learn that you should do unto others as you would have them do unto you. In network marketing, I have learned that you need to do unto others as you would have them do unto others.

It is the leaders who make the full-time income in our profession, but leadership is not the words you say, it is the actions you take. By the time you are making a full-time income in the business, you will be mentoring several people personally and coaching dozens more loosely, and touching/affecting tens of thousands internationally with your speeches, lessons, and trainings. It is important that you learn about the responsibility that being a mentor takes with it. In the last two chapters of the book, we will take a close look at what your business will look like in two to five years if you have learned and use these strategies properly and effectively.

The most crucial lessons I have learned in my career have come in this area. Mentor the leaders who come to you! Don't worry; you won't have to go out there trying to find people to mentor. They will beat down your door. Part of the strategy will be to learn how to create the right environment where everyone in your community has an equal chance to develop into a leader. By creating this community and giving your colleagues room to grow, you will create a platform where the proverbial "cream will rise to the top." When they rise, you will be ready.

I hope you are reading this book as a prospect or a new apprentice. If you are already in, you can start again. One of the first lessons I learned from my first mentor is that every day is a new day. Network marketing is the only profession on the planet where you can take a mulligan (golf term for a do-over stroke that you take when you don't like that your first shot landed up in a swamp). If you are already in, then use strategies in the book and start your business again right now.

Before we identify *The Most Important Minute*, let's take some time to look closely at why people join the business.

Chapter 2: Why Do Prospects Join?

"Leadership and learning are indispensable to each other."
John F. Kennedy

On hundreds of occasions I have asked groups of people this question: "What is the most important reason that someone joins the business with you?" Often the answers are because the product is good, they want more money, more free time, more time with their family, etc. These are all valid answers, but there is a much deeper, more correct, reason that is the same for everyone across the world. They join because of you, because they know you, like you, and trust you (KLT: know you, like you, trust you).

When I graduated from school, I had vivid dreams about traveling the world, driving the best car, living in a nice house, having the perfect job and the perfect family. What happened to that dream? I owned a mortgage company from 2002 until 2006. In that time our agents took applications from over 10,000 people looking for mortgage financing, and we generated hundreds of millions of dollars in fundings. Would it surprise you to learn that at least 90 percent of the people we took credit reports from were living one payday away from bankruptcy? That means that if their income was taken away tomorrow, they would survive 90 days at the most. Our society is failing at providing average people with financial and leadership education, and it has created a mess.

From time to time, we would ask our customers to fill out a questionnaire about their experience with their new mortgage. One of the questions we asked our clients was, "Where do you see yourself ten years from now?" The vast majority of people who answered this question responded that they were here! In other words, they didn't expect life to be much different. We also asked our clients to rate themselves on a scale of one to ten about where they were on the road to a perfect life (perfect being a 10). It probably wouldn't surprise you that the majority of respondents answered that they were a two or three. Well, if you are reading this book, you obviously decided that you want something more out of life. Congratulations!

Now don't get me wrong, we recognize that not all people are joining the team at a low point or stagnant point in their lives. We have a record number of successful people joining us because of the leadership education they receive in the business, and many teams and organizations are creating innovative leadership-based training communities designed to attract people to the business for reasons other then making money. So regardless of the prospect's initial reasons, they join because of you.

In *Being the Change*, you can learn how to create a complete cold prospecting strategy around the fact that people join because of you. So let's assume that the majority of prospects are joining at a point in life where they want more. If you would like to sign up more prospects in your business, you have to take the time to build a relationship with them, get them to KLT you. During the evaluation process, you have to help them to understand the opportunity, the product/service, the timing, and the compensation plan, but all of that plays second fiddle to you. The prospect stands a much better chance of joining if you build the relationship properly.

Think about your own original evaluation of the business, when you were a prospect. If you are new a brand-new distributor or a prospect yourself right now, I would bet my last dollar that this information is resonating with you.

Secret closing technique

Here is the biggest secret I can share about getting more people to join the business with you. I learned this skill while I was an interrogator. While doing interrogations, we would take the time to really get to know the bad guy. In law enforcement, we call it "Reid's Technique" or "Reid's Nine Steps." Take the time to get to know your prospect, ask lots of open-ended questions about them. People love to talk about themselves, so let them. As you focus on the prospect, don't interrupt them, express sincere interest (don't check your texts in the middle of the story), listen carefully, and ask follow-up questions to enhance conversation. The prospect will start to like you. You need to keep talking to them and asking questions until you find their reason, their why. An easy way to find their why is to remember the acronym F.O.R.M

(Family, Occupation, Recreation, and Mission). Cover those four bases and you will find their why.

During conversations, you will find the reason that the prospect needs your business, then it is just a matter of showing the prospect how your business will fulfill their need, and then it is sign up time! You can get an in-depth training on this technique by picking up the audio training *CD, How to Make Prospecting Second Nature* (www.nextcenturywealth.com).

A big part of getting someone to join the business is to get them dreaming again. When the

prospect joins the business, it is an indication that you have succeeded in helping the prospect believe that a ten out of ten quality of life is possible. When you first introduced the prospect to your opportunity, they were standing at the bottom of mountain.

As you build a friendship with them, introduce them to the various parts of your business, the compensation plan and the support, you have reignited that fire inside them, and they start dreaming again. They start climbing up the mountain of dreams. When they reach the peak of the mountain they are ready to join the business. They are standing on the summit, with their lungs full of the cool clean air, staring off into the vast endless space of possibility. As they sign their distributor application, and you enroll them in the business, they have hit the pinnacle.

Do you remember when you first caught the vision, when you stood on your summit? Do you remember how amazing it felt, seeing the unlimited potential of our profession? Joining the business is likely the most emotional decision you will ever make.

You have just found the most important minute.

Chapter 3: The Most Important Minute
Revealed

"Success is determined by the actions you take long after the emotion of the decision has passed."
Ken Dunn

Don't you wish that minute could last forever? Can you imagine standing on the summit of Mount Everest? You have just joined the business. You see all the potential in the world. You are more excited about your business than anything you have ever been excited about. You are not even sure what to do next, but you are fired up! If you've been around the profession for years and you don't remember the exhilaration of that first minute, the most important minute, then just trust me it is real and it is exactly how your new apprentice is feeling the minute they decide to join you in the business.

Have you ever signed someone up in the business, and they disappear without ever even opening their starter kit? Have you ever had someone join the business with you, quit months later, and blame you for their bad experience? Have you ever signed up someone new, asked them to write their names list or ask them to let you help them contact their first couple of prospects, and you are met with resistance by your new apprentice? Have you ever experienced an apprentice who signs up but avoids getting started? Did you join a network marketing business and quit two days later?

Now that we know what the most important minute in your network marketing career is, let's establish the right things to do in that single moment. When we learn how to use the most important minute properly, it will change the entire experience for you and your new apprentice. Also, when you learn how to properly use the most important minute, you will see a drastic difference in your answers to the questions that I asked on the previous page. We all know that if you want something big, you have to do something big. There are a significant number of people who never get started or disappear because the pain of change is greater than the pain of staying the same, and that's not your fault. However, understanding the strategies in The Most Important Minute can help create more success in your career.

The first thing we need to understand is that mountains have a point at the top and the other side can be a slippery slope. Have you ever heard of buyer's remorse, or the sober second thought? Joining a network marketing business is a purely emotional decision. There are a couple of reasons for all of the emotions:

1. *The barrier of entry is low enough:* If I were going to spend a million dollars on a new franchise, or $250,000 on a new business, I would take weeks/months to investigate the decision. Starting a network marketing business in a good company should cost between $250 and $1000. The sweet spot is $500 to $1000. Most people can join a company on a credit card, and even if they don't do anything and lose their initial investment, it is not the end of the world;

2. *People have an instant gratification mentality:* Even though we tell people over and over again that it takes two to five years

to build a full-time income in the profession, they get dummied up on the dreams and think they are super human. We can't stop people from talking about big money, and as long as we do, it will bring people in on that emotional rollercoaster called "get rich quick."

You have to act fast

So here you are standing at the top of the mountain, your dreams have completely clouded your judgment, you are flying your own jet, sailing around the world, living on the beach making beach money *(read Jordan Adler's book Beach Money)*, but what next? Would you believe me if I told you that the vast majority of sponsors (or enrollers) have never been taught what to do with someone the minute they join? Here's the problem. It's called adrenalin dump, and it's what happens to the vast majority of people who join the business within minutes of them getting started.

Within minutes of joining the business, your apprentice is starting to get worried. Think about that mountain that they are standing on. The down side of the mountain is steep and it can be a nasty fall. If we agree that we are at a ten/ten the minute we join the business, then we have already slumped back down to a seven/ten within seventy-two hours, and it gets worse from there. Once the apprentice starts falling, it is hard to come back.

We have a golden rule in our team: never go to sleep with an application sitting on the desk. I have met dozens of people over the years who will get their prospect to the summit, take the application, and then wait days before they actually sign their new partner up. The apprentice is already six to seven/ten before the application is even submitted. If the prospect is ready to give you their application at midnight, then you have to be ready to get him/her started at midnight.

It's not just about being a great recruiter; it's also about being a great starter

Writing this book has made me think of the many people I have stranded at the side of the road in the industry. If you are reading this book and you were one of the first people I sponsored into the profession, I am truly sorry, I owe you lunch and a sincere apology. The fact is no one taught me how to be a great starter. I could sign people up at will, but I had no idea what to do next.

I remember getting so frustrated that all these people would sign up with me, but that no one was doing anything. I was the only one working. I couldn't find anyone like me. Have you heard or thought these things before? It is a reality that your excitement will drop significantly within seventy-two hours of joining the business, unless you use the most important minute properly.

Section 2: Keep Them In

Chapter 4: You're In, Now What?

"Leadership is the capacity to translate vision into reality."
Warren G. Bennis

I hope someone gave you this book the minute you joined the business because they knew it was the Most Important Minute. Even if that is not the case, we have to understand that someone has a much higher chance of success if we can ride and sustain that emotional high. If we can keep people at a ten/ten through the first seventy-two hours, then they will climb higher and not fall at all. In the next chapter, we will learn a technique about how to keep them climbing the five levels of belief and ensure they stay in forever. But first let's learn exactly what to do in the first minute, hours, and days after they sign to ensure higher levels of success, and create duplication in our team.

One of my heroes in our profession, Art Jonak always reminds people not to be so absolute, but I have to be that here just one time. In our team, you must get your apprentice started exactly this way.

It was around my five-thousandth hour in the profession that I finally started learning how to get someone started properly. The most important lesson I have ever learned about using the most important minute effectively is to start now!

The minute I sign up a new rep in the business, I go see them immediately. If they live within a four-hour drive, I will change my plans that day and drive to see them. You should always have three to four extra starter kits from your company or team on hand, as well as getting-started tools and product samples. As soon as they have finished giving me their credit card information, I book a time that day to drop off their starter kit, getting-started tools, and their product samples. We have an agreement that as soon as their order arrives, they will give it back to me. That way we always have kits in rotation.

You need to provide constant, immediate support for your apprentice to prevent buyer's remorse. Any delays in responding to your new apprentice's needs will result in him/her second-guessing the decision to sign up. Keep the positive emotions flowing; help your new apprentice stay on the mountain peak. Try it next time you sign someone up. Before you hang up the phone, ask them when you can stop by to drop off their getting-started kit. You'll be amazed! They will meet you 99 percent of the time. If not today, they certainly will meet first thing tomorrow.

The most amazing part is that as soon as you book the appointment, give them some homework and they will do it. *Okay, I'll see you at 4 p.m. with your starter kit and product. Before, I get there, go through the getting-started training in the back office and make some notes. I'll look forward to hearing what you think.*

By the time you show up at the house, your apprentice has already devoured the entire back office, searched the product, all the corporate officers, and the top leaders online, and can tell you how often the bonus checks come. They are still excited. The technique worked. You have succeeded in maintaining the positive emotions.

Remember, your apprentice is looking for a leader. In Kevin Hall's Book Aspire, on page 27, Kevin shares the origin of the word leader:

"The word is Indo-European, and that it is derived from two words. The first part ---l-e-a--- means path, and the second part ---d-e-r--- means finder. A leader is a pathfinder."

Always remember that your apprentice sees you as the pathfinder so show them the way. In the same way, if you are just starting or restarting, then find a pathfinder. Every apprentice needs a leader and a mentor. If you are in that position, then this book can guide you, but I would encourage you to look up and find someone that is in your success line, or upline, that can help guide you.

This first meeting and getting started is crucial. The closer it is to the most important minute, the better. If you have ever had someone disappear from the business or never get started, there was probably a lack of understanding of the most important minute. If you're just getting started then follow the list mentioned below and you will make it.

Assemble the business binder/getting-started kit

As soon as I show up at the house/ appointment/ meeting, I take out the business binder. This is the holy grail of success so treat it respectfully. Ensure that you go through all the pages with your apprentice, and take the time to watch the DVDs that come with it. Take a few minutes to talk about all of the tools that come with the kit, and review the best use of each tool.

Next step is to fill out the information sheet and help your apprentice determine their short, medium, and long-term income goals. Make sure that the income goals that they are setting are attainable. If your apprentice sets a goal of earning $10,000 USD/month in six months from now, but can only work 10 hours per week, they are setting themselves up for failure. Help the apprentice set other goals that are applicable and realistic. Then take some time to discuss the why. This is crucial. Your why should make you cry. It may take some time for your apprentice to really discover that deep-rooted reason, so don't push them too hard; it is better to set the stage.

Make a list

The next thing I always do with my new apprentice is help them make a list. In a good getting-started package, there will always be a set of memory joggers (list of conventional professions, occupations, and pastimes designed to jog one's memory). I tell my apprentice we need to make a list of fifty people they know, like, and trust (KLT goes both ways).

It is important to start the list with all the best friends and family members. I have to tell you, I have had many people say they don't want to talk to their friends and family because they want to make money first. They say they know they will join if they are making money. If you don't talk to those people first you will never make money, and you will create some really bad blood when you are successful.

I started my network marketing career in 2003. I was one of those lucky (Labour Under Correct Knowledge) people who made money right away. I quit my job at the police service in Ottawa, Canada after only four months in the business. I had money coming in from other avenues, but I was already earning comma checks in my MLM company.

It is customary to meet with the chief of police on your way out. It's called an exit interview. After the interview I was riding the elevator down to the locker room when one of my colleagues jumped in. Paul didn't even say hi to me. We had worked together two years earlier, but now we were working in two different units. I was investigating attempted murders and he was investigating auto thefts.

Because we were on opposite shifts in totally different crime areas, we rarely saw each other anymore. After two floors passed without a word, I asked Paul what was wrong. He said, "I heard you're quitting today. You hit the jackpot in some new business." Instantly, my prospecting bells starting ringing, and I said, "Yeah, Paul, it's awesome. You have to check it out. The boys are all doing it." As the elevator door opened, he turned, looked me right in the face, and said, "If you were really my friend, I would have been one of the first people you called." He walked off and I have never spoken to him since. Moral to the story: Don't leave anyone off the list.

Once the list is done, we book the business launch event at the apprentice's home. Some cultures and people don't want to use their home for this meeting. It's okay. There just needs to be a launch meeting booked within the first fourteen days of the most important minute. You could try a meeting hall or your house. It is a crucial point in getting started right. If you are the pathfinder, then you will conduct the first meeting for your apprentice.

The first five are the most important five

Now that the list is built and the meeting is booked, the next step is somewhat controversial, but it is almost mandatory in our community. While I am with my new apprentice, I will personally call the first five prospects and book one-on-one meetings. Remember, your new partner is your apprentice. The definition of apprentice is on page 12.

The first five people on their list are the most important people. I make the call so that the apprentice can hear the words, the confidence, the tone, and because it is what I want the apprentice to do with his/her first apprentice. Duplication! Network marketing is the purest lead by example platform on the planet. It is an entire volunteer workforce. Your apprentice is more likely to do what they see you doing than to do what you tell them to.

When you call those first five people for your apprentice, your conversation should go something like this:

"Hi Mike. This is [insert your name]. I am sitting here with your buddy Steve. Steve and I are starting a new business together and we want to bring you some information. We are fired up about it, and Steve said you would be interested. When's a good time to drop by? Okay 3 p.m. is great. Hey, before we get there, you may want to look at our website. Do you have a pen? Okay here it is…… I'll see you then. Here's Steve."

As the pathfinder, you should do this for the top five prospects on your apprentice's list. If you are new, and don't have a pathfinder, find one and ask for help with the first five prospects.

Now Steve and I are meeting with the first five prospects, and Steve will call the remaining people on the list to come to the in-home meeting. Again, as the journeyman, I will even make the first few invitation calls so that the apprentice can get a good feel for it.

As the pathfinder, I will do those first five one-on-one meetings and let Steve sit back and watch. If Steve wants to interject or add value to the conversations, never stop that. Always remember it is Steve's friend, not yours. I know that is obvious, but my first mentor actually told me to sit back and shut up. If I wanted him doing the meeting then I shouldn't interfere. Truth be told, it is the same thing

I said to some of my first new people. If I had my time back I would have done it all different.

Review the back office with your apprentice

How did they ever do network marketing before the internet? Most companies today have great online and back office systems that are very self-explanatory. Don't ever assume that your new apprentice is a savvy techy. Take time to go through the entire back office with your new apprentice, and make sure you show them where all the customer service information is for all of the questions they have. Also encourage them to call the company if there are any general company related questions.

In the twenty-first century of network marketing, many communities are being built in the field. Groups of people are coming together with similar ideals and passions, and creating some of the greatest movements towards financial freedom that the world has ever seen. If you are lucky enough to have both a great company and a great team environment, then make sure you take the time to help your apprentice see and understand all of the team dynamics and any team specific training materials.

We need great audio/literature leadership training systems

Towards the end of the first meeting, I will spend time making sure the apprentice gets turned on to the right CD and books, and understands all of the benefits of being in a leadership learning environment.

Get plugged in immediately

Nothing beats a sense of urgency. You have already created a sense of urgency with your new apprentice by coming over the same day, so keep it going. If you are lucky enough to have an established weekly meeting going on in your market, attend the meetings and ensure your apprentice attends. Make sure your apprentice is tuned into the conference calls, weekly meetings, and major events going on in your team.

Have your new apprentice commit to the next major convention and buy their ticket right there. Becoming a ticket holder keeps your new apprentice looking forward and thinking positively about their new business. In chapter 10, we will dig into the importance of going to every event.

Off to the races

Now you know exactly what the most important minute is and how to properly use it. If you follow the most important minute strategies to start your own business and pass it on to every apprentice you help get started, you will see great duplication start in your group.

Imagine if every new apprentice in your downline did exactly what we have learned in the past few pages. Here's another secret: they will duplicate the most important minute strategy because now they know what it is and how it works. There are a couple of things that we have to clarify here.

No pathfinder, no mentor. If you are on your own without a good sponsor, it doesn't change the plan. This book can be your pathfinder.

Long distance sponsoring. You can still use the same strategies with your new apprentice even if they are on the other side of the state, country, or world. Most getting-started manuals are electronic now and on the website, so you can still have the first meeting, find the why, set goals, make the list, book the in-home, and call the first five using the telephone and the internet.

The most crucial point in this strategy is that every second counts. You have to get your new apprentice into motion right away. Don't wait even one day. Every day you wait increases the likelihood that they will never start. Be a positive statistic, not a negative one.

Let's move on and look at strategy for building belief.

Chapter 5: Five Levels of Belief

"The key to successful leadership today is influence,
not authority."
Ken Blanchard

In chapter 2, we discovered the biggest reason that people, in general join the business. Prospects join the business because of you. If you take the time build a relationship with your prospect, they are much more likely to join your business. If you think about it, you are the only variable in the recruiting process.

There are really five to six things that we focus on when we introduce a prospect to the business. We want to make sure that they get excited about: the product/service, the timing, the compensation plan, the owners/principles, and expansion plans. Each of these points is the same for everyone. The points are static. The only part of the process you can affect is the storyteller.

Have you ever wondered why some people struggle for years to sign up their first rep, while others seem to sponsor people at will? The only variable is you. So you have to get great at telling the story and becoming believable. Inevitably, the prospect believes in you when they join. If you leave the apprentice there, believing in you, it will end up causing you a lot of pain. If the apprentice decides to stop trying right now and quits, then they will know nothing else other than to blame you.

Have you ever had new people stop, or quit, or get frustrated and blame you? "My sponsor didn't help me; my sponsor lied to me; my sponsor didn't follow through." Well, if you understand the most important minute strategy to building belief, you will radically change the blame game and help your apprentice move forward. We all know that if we are going to earn full-time income in the profession, we have to build belief in ourselves; we have to believe that we can do it; and we have to believe it is possible.

Houston, we have a problem!

The problem is that most prospects have stopped dreaming. Do you remember when you finished school full of dreams? You expected to live in a nice house, drive a great car, take two vacations a year, and not want for anything. What happened? Life happened. It is really hard to believe in yourself when you've stopped dreaming.

If you want to get someone to believe in themselves and take the blame off of you, then you have to help them believe in themselves. It is a really simple process to helping your apprentice build belief. It will take about six to eight weeks after the apprentice enrolls.

There are five steps to belief.

To get an apprentice to believe in themselves, you first have to get them to believe in the product/service, the company, the profession, and then they will begin to believe in themselves.

Step 1: You

When a prospect joins they are believing mostly in you and very little in the opportunity or themselves.

THE FIVE STEPS TO BELIEF

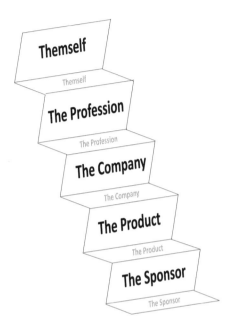

We have to change this, or it will cause trouble later.

Step 2: The product

As soon as I sponsor a new partner, I start talking a lot about the product. I continue to focus on the product for the next couple of weeks. I get them onto product conference calls and do two-way calls with teammates to let the apprentice hear lots of information about the product. I even feed my apprentice lots of product literature. I know when the apprentice is starting to believe in the product because he/she will start to talk a lot about the product themselves.

Step 3: The company

Once they start talking regularly about the product, then I switch my focus to the company. I regularly talk about the owners and the corporate officers. I will show the apprentice records that the company is doing well, is stable, etc. I direct the apprentice to conference calls, recordings and tools where the apprentice is heavily exposed to all aspects of the company. I know that the apprentice's belief in the company is growing because he/she starts to focus on the company.

Step 4: The profession

Now that the apprentice is talking about the company and the product, I realize it is the right time to introduce the apprentice to this amazing profession called direct sales. The very first thing that I do is get each apprentice to subscribe to the direct sales top periodical, Networking Times. Publishers/Owners Chris and Josephine Gross are true guardians of the profession, and they publish a world-caliber periodical that showcases the best practices, news, and experiences of the world's top community builders. You can get your own subscription at www.networkingtimes.com. Tell them Ken sent you!

I help my apprentice understand that our company is part of an amazing emerging profession that is growing faster than real estate or the internet. Over 490 billion dollars in sales was done by over thirty-five thousand companies around the world in 2009. It is definitely something to be proud of.

Step 5: Themselves

It is almost magical watching what happens by following this process. As the apprentice starts to understand the power of the profession, I can see the confidence soar. Now that the apprentice believes in the product, company, and profession, they become more outgoing, more ready to engage in conversation on a moments notice, and more comfortable talking about the details of the opportunity. Without even focusing on it, the belief in themselves goes through the roof. Sometimes you can only achieve the things you most want by not focusing on them. Try this technique with your next apprentice. You will be amazed by the difference in them, and they will stop blaming you.

Section 3: Move Them Along!

Chapter 6: The Apprentice Gets Their License

"Education is the mother of leadership."
Wendell Willkie

As you start to go out and do meetings with your apprentice, build belief and take action together, your apprentice will start spreading their wings. It is fun to watch it happen. If you are an apprentice in the business, don't wait for the test or the grades. When you feel comfortable talking to people, do it! The sooner you go out and become independent, the sooner you will begin to earn money. You have to become a leader.

In the first couple of weeks, you should stay close to your new apprentice, building your friendship, and talking several times a day. Doing meetings together should be a regular occurrence. When you are meeting people together be respectful of each other, and always remember the prospect you are meeting is likely a friend of the apprentice so let the apprentice be involved in the conversation. At the same time, if you are the apprentice then let your mentor do all the talking. This will give you a chance to take notes and study the mentor, and it will tell your prospect that you have tons of respect for the mentor. Leadership is the action you take, not the things you say.

When you are showing the business to a new prospect keep it simple and never change the script. The biggest mistake apprentices make is that they get bored and feel they have to jazz up the presentation. Always remember that it is a different prospect and there is no need to change anything, ever. Be wary of the people who feel that things have to be changing.

You are ready!

Once you feel that you can do it, then do it! There is never going to be a perfect presentation. They only way to get great telling the story is to first get good. The only way to get good at telling a story is to first be bad. Once you have done four to five presentations (one-on-one's, group meetings, hotel meetings, webinars, etc.) with your sponsor, upline, and business partner then you are ready to do it on your own. Make sure you use the tools that your team/upline is suggesting, and get out there and talk to people. In my book, *Being the Change*, you will learn several proven techniques to generate limitless leads so that you can keep starting over.

Never stop prospecting

The only thing in common with all elite-level earners in our profession is they never stop prospecting, and neither should you. Now the amount of prospecting you do will decrease as your income goes up. You will need to use more of your time building depth and helping your leaders. I have put together a little chart that gives you an understanding of a good baseline of time spent recruiting at different income levels.

Monthly Income	% of time spent prospecting
0 - $5,000	90%
$5,000 - $10,000	70%
$10,000 - $25,000	50%
$25,000 & up	40%

If you want to create duplication in your group, your team has to have an example to follow.

The speed of the team will only ever be half the speed of the leader.

You are now on your way to freedom. Another similarity that the big guns in the business have in common is that they are experts at keeping themselves motivated. They are constantly chasing the prize.

The last point that I need to talk to you about in this chapter is the fact that different people take different amounts of time to truly become independent and make their business profitable. We have all heard the cliche "the only people that fail are the ones that quit." It is a great saying, but often leaves people thinking, "Okay I get it, but why?" The reality is that to become a true independent business owner and lead a team, you are going to have to develop a new skills, and it will take time. Remember earlier in the book we talked about outliers, 10,000 hours. You cannot circumvent the experience piece.

Some people will take two to three years to sponsor their first partner; others will sponsor two to three in their first month. Take your time as an apprentice seriously. You have to develop real business leadership skills; you have to refine your ability to build relationships. We will talk in more details about this in the next couple of chapters. You will not move from apprentice to leader (mentor) until you start developing these skills, so embrace it, love it, and live it.

Chapter 7: Keep Your Eyes on the Prize!

"The life blood of the business is the new blood."
Mark Yarnell

We have now established that success is not a lottery win, but that is not to say you shouldn't play the lottery in your company! A good company will be constantly running performance-based contest. The prizes will vary from cash incentives to bonuses.

As I look back at my career, I realize that I have always focused on winning every contest my company has held. In my first year in network marketing, the team I was a part of had a year-long contest. In the contest, you would get points for sponsoring new partners, for your rank advancement, for helping people in your team to rank advance, and a couple of other things. First place in the contest was a brand-new Porsche Boxster. The winner of the contest would win the car outright. The day I heard about the contest, I went out and bought a poster of the Boxster and hung it in my office above my desk. I also went to the department of motor vehicle and bought a personalized license plate that said MLMPAYS, and hung that license plate below the picture.

Next I created a tracking form on my desk on a piece of paper where I wrote down every point I got, including the date and the description of how I got the points. Fourteen months later there was a brand-new Porsche Boxster sitting in my driveway. I learned a valuable lesson, and won a new Porsche, in that experience.

It will take a couple of years to see consistent income start to come in. Network marketing is no different than any other business. I have always focused on winning every contest my company has ever run. If you are in a great company, they will be constantly running some type of performance-based contest. The smartest corporate management teams design their contest around some simple criteria.

1. Your contest should reward the right behavior–recruiting new distributors. If your company has multiple options for joining, as the FTC in the United States encourages, then you should expect higher contest rewards to those that recruit at the highest packages. The contest should also reward for gathering customers

2. Your contest should reward people for helping their teammates promote to the next level.

3. The contest will reward everyone for a minimum amount of behavior, and also reward the top performers.

A lot of network marketing company contest have prizes that are trips to exotic destinations. My family and I have been on more then twenty luxurious trips to many of the world's greatest beaches. The memories that have been created, and the friendships that have been made, will be cherished forever. Thank you, network marketing!

The greatest contests do not have cash prizes. The prizes that create experiences serve both as a reward for accomplishment and a dream-building experience. As a brand-new apprentice, how would you like to go on an all-expense paid trip to Bora Bora, or a wild animal safari in the Sahara, or a ten-day cruise of the Mediterranean? Throughout your career, make sure you are always on the leader board. Win the contest, or rank high. Even if you are having a slow start, at least focus on the contest and try. This is the best example to set, and the true hallmark of a leader, a mentor!

Take the contest seriously

Here are a couple of suggestions for getting the most out of a network marketing contest.

1. Start on day one. Decide to take the contest seriously, and start participating the day the contest starts.

2. Set up for success. Most contests will be over a period of time. You have to keep yourself engaged every day. Create a dream board, or a reminder of the contest that includes pictures of the prizes and pictures of your family. Put this dream board on the wall in front of your telephone

3. Create your own tracking form. Print a copy of the rules and make a spreadsheet. Keep track of your own points so that you can verify against the company's tracking.

4. Talk it up. Whenever you are around teammates, talk about the contest and create rivalry.

5. Create training. Include how to win trainings into your training events

6. Learn a lesson. Regardless of how you make out, reflect afterwards and pick out lessons learned and points to improve on.

Only one person comes in first. Good contests are designed so that with a specific amount of effort many people can win the prize. Because you have to get good at your business, you may start off slow and not do well in the contests. Don't get frustrated, but rather get fired up about the next contest. A great idea for your team would be to have a party or event afterwards to celebrate everyone who even participated.

Chapter 8: Never Miss an Event!

"Leaders don't create followers,
they create more leaders."
Tom Peters

I joined the business in November 2003 and got off to a pretty good start. By the fourth month, I had forty people in my team. The company I joined was having an international convention of over 600 people in my home city. Everyone around me was excited and buying tickets. Every time I turned around, I walked right into a conversation about the convention. It was driving me crazy!

At that time, I was investigating murders and writing mortgages. Network marketing was something extra I was doing for fun. My friends and I used to make fun of what we were doing. I had no intention of going to the convention. Why did I need to? I made $2800 USD in my third month in the business. What could I learn at that event? Yes, I was arrogant.

I am very thankful that I had a mentor that first year who really understood the business. He had already been in the profession for over a decade, and at the time he was making over $100,000 per month. He happened to live in the same city. One day he asked me why I was not going to the convention. I told him I didn't need to learn anything, and that I had lots going on. My mentor told me I had to be there as I was going to win one of the big recruiting awards and was going to get a chance to speak on stage. Boy, did he know how to get me excited. He also suggested that I needed to get all forty of my people there as they would get really fired up when they saw me win the award. Best way to motivate an egomaniac? Tell him he is going to get a trophy in front of 600 people. Thankfully, I have changed.

I ended up convincing my friends to come. It was the best lesson I have ever learned in our profession. At the convention, I met people from all over the world. I had no idea so many people were doing this business. There were people from all walks of life, including doctors, lawyers, dentists, CEOs of

Fortune 500 companies, etc. I was also blown away at what I learned about the products in our company. I got to meet the product formulator. He had put his whole life into the products. The products were helping people all over the world. I was elated to be on the stage, and realized I wanted everyone in my team to feel that same thing.

The month after the convention, my team tripled and my income went from $2800 to over $10,000 a month. Now that is an extraordinary example of the reason to attend events, but it proves an invaluable point. If you want to make a full-time income in the profession, you have to attend all of the events.

An event describes everything from our weekly open meetings, to Saturday trainings, webinars, conference calls, quarterly events, major conventions, etc. Since that first convention, I have never missed an event, and you shouldn't either.

We are in the ticket-selling business

The importance of attending events cannot be overstated. Network marketing is an independent business. We all live in our own towns, with our own circles of influence. As we build the business, we are constantly trying to balance a lot of outside forces, ranging from your relatives and their stinkin' thinking, to the critics, to the stress of work, bills and family issues. You will have days where you say, "I have to keep going." Attending the events gives you a chance to recharge the jets. You are around all of the positive people in the team, learning about the company and products, while developing the leadership skills that you will need to win. Getting to the convention will keep you in the business.

In our team we have major conventions every four months, monthly regional events, and weekly open meetings to ensure that we keep our teammates in a constant supportive positive environment. If you are going to build a successful business in the team, you have to attend all the events. Remember leadership is revealed in the examples you set. If you go to the events, so will your people. If you are in a good community, they should constantly be selling tickets to the next event and you should always be a ticket holder.

Ticket holders are guaranteed to win!

In our community, we have many special incentives to be a ticket holder all the time. We are always selling the tickets to the next major event at the current major event. We have realized that if someone owns a ticket to the next event, they are 95 percent likely to go. If they constantly are in possession of a ticket, then they will never quit. Our theory is that by doing a lot of special events for ticket holders only, we are adding value; our people see that they are getting their money's worth before they even get to the major.

The moral of the story: get your ticket to the next event. Set the example in your team. Most people wait until the last minute to buy their ticket. They always say that it is a budget thing and can't afford it. But isn't it funny how those same people have the same financial problems and still manage to get their tickets.

It's all in your mind

Find a way to buy your ticket now. Don't even worry about how you are going to get there, or how you are going to afford to get there. We can help you with shared accommodations and travel. My whole goal with my new apprentice is to get them to buy their ticket the day they join. I know if they do it, then they will be at the convention. You should always be promoting an event in your team. Events come in many shapes and sizes. In a well-organized community, there will be webinars, conference calls, weekly open meetings, monthly Saturday training events, quarterly regional events, and national/international conventions every four months.

If you are an apprentice right now and just getting started, attend all of the events. This starts with doing your weekly meeting every week! The people who are not willing to truly be an apprentice will hate the idea of going to the weekly opens every week, and will try to rationalize it by saying they don't have a prospect this week, so why bother. This is shallow thinking that will result in a much harder time getting through the apprentice process.

Attending events has so many benefits:

- You increase your chances of associating with the right people.

- You will learn more about your opportunity faster.

- You will stay up to speed on any new announcement.

- You will have a much easier time building belief.

- You will become more confident in the opportunity.

It's not a coincidence that everyone making over $1,000 per month attends the events!

Chapter 9: Front Row Attitude

*"Leadership is practiced not so much in words
as in attitude and in actions."*
Harold S. Genee

As I entered the room at my first convention, I felt like I was at a rock concert. It wasn't because of the lights, stage, or loud music. I was amazed at the mad dash for the front of the room. The convention started at 9 a.m. Friday morning. At 7:30 a.m. there were people lining up. As I walked passed them on my way to breakfast, I thought to myself, "These guys are crazy." By 8:30 a.m., there were hundreds of people standing body to body in the entrance to the ballroom.

For a minute, I slipped back into my policeman's role and thought about breaking into crowd control mode, but then realized every one of them was excited and happy. These crazy network marketers were enjoying the mayhem. Then I experienced one of the most powerful events that occurred in the team. In a second, all four sets of doors opened to loud dance music, and everyone started running. It was like someone had shot the starters pistol at the 100 meter finals at the Olympics. The entire crowd started running for the front of the room. I soon realized that the hysteria was caused by hundreds of people who all wanted to be in the front row.

That first convention was amazing and taught me many lessons that still serve me today. The most important lesson was that at every event you go to, you have to be in the front row. In fact, the lesson is bigger then the event. If you are going to succeed in going from apprentice to mentor, and make a full-time income in the team, then you have to develop a front row attitude.

Remember how back in chapter 2 I said most people are walking through life at a two out of ten on the dreamers scale. Most people come into the business on the bottom rungs of the ladder. As a leader, it is your job to pour energy, fun, and excitement into the lives of everyone around you. A front row attitude is an attitude where you look at the glass at half full on the stormy days. You remind yourself that the sun will come out tomorrow, that driving in a car for six hours means six hours to study leadership and listen to great CDs, that when something bad happens to you, you always see it as a great lesson.

In order to build a profitable business, you have to lead people. The people that you lead are all volunteers. They don't have to do what you say. They will do what you do. There is only one way to lead volunteers: through your example! In my first year of network marketing, I was a dictator. I used to demand and order people around. We know what happened at the end of the first year. When I focused on being a better person, and loving people, my entire world changed and my business exploded. During my years in policing, I always thought the worst of people. My outlook on life was dark and jaded. As I worked on creating a better me, I started to see the world in an entirely different way. We have to realize that leadership is not determined by the direction you give, but by the example you set. People don't follow people; they follow examples.

We say that you have to develop a front row attitude because the attitude resembles the attitudes of those hundreds of people rushing to the front seats. Whenever you are at an event, it is crucial to sit in the front row, take lots of notes (even if it is your thousandth time seeing the same presentation), and pay attention. Other people in your group will see this and do the same thing. When I am at an event, I can tell the growth of the business, and the strength of the community, by what the top leaders are doing. If I go into an event and see that all the top leaders are sitting in the first couple of rows, then it is an indication that these are servant leaders who are concerned about setting the right example for their teammates, and consequently the business will grow well. On the other hand, if all the leaders are hanging out in the back of the room, engaged in side conversation, or are not even in the room but running little side meetings, etc., then this indicates that dysfunction and ego has set into the group, and no community is flourishing.

As a mentor, you need to set the example and have a front row attitude, both at the event and in everyday life. The mentor should be constantly loving and praising teammates. If you are an apprentice, building your 10,000 hours, then always sit in the front row, in everything you do.

As an apprentice, make sure that you sign up for the CD/book standing order the day you join. The CDs have the best speeches on leadership, personal development, and business building strategies, and the books are the greatest books on growing a better business and a better you. To develop a front row attitude, you must learn. The CDs/books are the most important part of that process. When you get the standing order every month, make sure you read the book and listen to the CDs every day. You will develop the front row attitude by studying these materials.

A front row attitude is contagious

Your attitude will determine your altitude! It was Jim Rohn who first uttered those words. Rohn explained that by having a good attitude all the time, even on the bad days, you would attract good things to you. This is 100 percent true and has been proven over and over. An apprentice needs to understand that the tone of a community will be set by the attitude of the leader. When your team sees that you are 100 percent positive 100 percent of the time, they will start to act the same way.

Developing a front row attitude is the first step in becoming a leader. Leadership is determined by the example you set for other people. You want to become a leader because it is the leaders that make the money!

THE MOST IMPORTANT MINUTE

Chapter 10: The Leaders Make the Money

*"The greatest leader of all is one
who learns to lead self first."*
Ken Dunn

In order to make a full-time income in your network marketing business you will have to develop specific leadership skills. It was once said that they hardest organization to ever lead is the one that is not looking to be lead. Every single person that joins your network marketing business is a volunteer and is not looking for a boss. One of the common reasons that millions of new people are flocking to our profession is that they are looking to get rid of all of their bosses.

So how do we lead people that don't want to be lead? That is a question I wish someone had answered for me in my first year. Having grown up in the policing world, I had a jaded perspective on leadership. Looking back, I can tell you how not to lead in network marketing. I used to be the greatest example of authoritarian leadership. I told people what to do, never praised them, and never encouraged them. This style of leadership is the biggest reason my business collapsed in 2004. I have spent every second since then refining me. I have realized that I can't even begin to understand how to lead others until I learn to lead myself.

Right around the same time my business collapsed in 2004, I was working my network marketing business in Mexico City when I met an incredible man named Juan Carlos Barrios. A friend asked me to have lunch with a prospect couple, Juan Carlos (JC) and Hortensia (Horte) Barrios. We met for lunch on the roof of a five-star hotel. I remember the day as if it were yesterday. It was a turbulent period for me. Back in Canada, my business was falling apart and my mind was all over the place.

Several years later, I had the great fortune to meet one of the world's greatest leadership educators and authors, John C Maxwell in Dallas, Texas. I was invited to speak at the same leadership event he was the keynote speaker at. Following the seminar, we all attended Elevate Life Church in Frisco, Texas with Pastor Keith Craft. John Maxwell was asked to preach there. During this sermon, John uttered words that have stuck with me ever since: "When God has a problem, he always has a person." In 2004, the problem was me and I needed to fix it. The person was Juan Carlos, and I feel blessed to have JC and Horte in my life.

Since then, Juan Carlos has provided me with an impeccable example of leadership to follow. During your apprenticeship in network marketing you are going to have to learn to be a better leader. My greatest piece of advice to this end will be to find someone in your support line, in the team that is already achieving the levels of success you hope to, and ask them to mentor you.

Every leader is a follower

The biggest lesson I have learned in leadership is that every great leader in the world attributes their success to coaching from a mentor. When I was young and naive, I thought that if anyone was going to succeed it was going to be completely on their own. What I have come to understand is that no great leader ever does it on their own. You can learn a great deal of the leadership lessons I have learned by reading *Being the Change.* This section is about the relevance of leadership development in getting started, and successfully building your network marketing business. Before you can learn to lead, and become a mentor, you first have to successfully complete your apprenticeship.

If you follow *The Most Important Minute* strategy to getting started, you will definitely get your business started in the best way possible. If you use strategies to get other people started, you will create duplication in your group. The most important part of this idea is to take action. Don't wait for someone else to tell you. One of the only things in common with all full-time income earners is that they independently take action. You have signed up to be an independent distributor.

The first step to becoming a leader is to start making money. The first step to making money is to take action. Leadership is not the things you say, but rather the things you do. Perhaps a little twist on one of the Ten Commandments fits here. In the Bible, we know to do unto others as you would have them do unto you. In network marketing, you have to do unto others as you would have them do unto others. It is your example that will set you free.

In the industry, you will have access to the greatest leadership development training program on the planet. Make sure you subscribe to the CD and book program. Every leader in the business making full-time income subscribes to the leadership CD program and listens to those CDs several times over. People are going to join the business with you if they know you, like you, and trust you. So the most important aspect of leadership you need to develop is you. You have to make yourself the most likeable you can be. It is crucial to look in a mirror and examine yourself, both inwardly and outwardly. People will most likely follow you if they look up to you. Think about that for a minute. Who is more likely to be followed? The physically fit, well-dressed business professional, or the unhealthy, overweight cigarette-smoking guy wearing the blue jeans and the T-Shirt? Who is more likely to be followed? The unshaven guy dropping f-bombs, or the clean cut gentleman who is careful of his language and always speaks well.

Leadership in network marketing is about the example you set, the actions you take, and the behaviors you model. As an apprentice, the best use of your time is to learn how to think, how to act, how to present. As you are out talking to people about your business opportunity, the chances of them joining you are directly related to the time you have spent working on you. Don't worry if you realize you have some work to do on yourself; you are already ahead of the masses. It took me thirty years to realize that I was at the bottom and not at the top.

The size of your group and your paycheck will be directly proportional to the size of your heart.

One of the many books you will want to read along the way is *The Fred Factor by Mark Sanborn*. This is a great book in which the author expresses the importance of servant leadership in business by profiling his mail delivery man, Fred. Fred the postman goes far beyond what is expected, and in doing so, sets the example for the world on the true art of leadership. On page 111, Sanborn talks about attitude. In order to develop into a leader, you have to develop your own front row attitude. It's no coincidence that all these chapters fit together. Here are Sanborn's thoughts on attitude:

> *Here's an interesting dilemma: You can do all the right things, but if they're done for the wrong reasons or with the wrong attitude, your efforts will be short-circuited.*

What won't work: Acting like Fred because you feel you have to. What will work: Acting like Fred because you want to.

Attitude colors everything you and I do in life.

A positive attitude allows you to see the things you undertake as an opportunity, not an obligation.

A positive attitude looks for the best, not the worst, in circumstances.

A positive attitude is "can-do" not "must-do."

A positive attitude is hopeful, not pessimistic.

On your way from apprentice to mentor, you will have to become a better leader. Becoming a better leader is about developing a front row attitude, becoming the best you that you can (inwardly and outwardly), developing habits of listening to the best CDs and reading the best books, setting the right example, and trying to find ways to help someone every day.

In a good network marketing business, there will be a huge emphasis on leadership development.

Make sure you take part. In our business, perhaps more so than any other industry, servant leadership is key to success. When your team truly knows that you care more about them and their success than your own success, they will be loyal to you and your company, and you will create a massive walk-away income.

The moral to the story is that the secret to learning the leadership skills is to not worry about learning the leadership skills. In the beginning, work on being the best person you can be to others and serve people every day; the rest will happen on its own.

The biggest lesson I have ever learned about leadership in network marketing is that the leaders, the men and women making full-time income, don't wait for others to tell them what to do. They take action! As quickly as possible, you must become an independent leader. That means you have to go out there and build your business. You have to go do your own one-on-one presentations, you have to arrange your in-home meetings, and if you wait for others to do it for you, you will not win. As Randy Gage says, "you need to become a Victor and not a Victim." The victors are the ones that read this book and others like it, and take actions, never give up, work on themselves the most, love people where they are at,

don't worry about the ones that are not doing enough,
and keep moving forward. Become a leader!

Chapter 11: The Power of the Bamboo Tree

"Notice that the stiffest tree is most easily cracked, while the bamboo or willow survives by bending with the wind."

Bruce Lee

Your goal is to create a business with thousands of independent leaders in it that only call you to thank you.

Your goal is to eventually create a business that you work on for about four to five hours per week, and all of that time is spent calling people to tell them how much you appreciate them and love them.

You goal is to be making those calls from your beach house in the Mediterranean, or your winter home in Brazil.

Your goal is to create incredible life-long relationships with people all over the world, and you just happen to make money from their efforts. But the friendships are now so strong that even if the money was gone the friendship would still be there.

These are your goals and there are many more, but how can it actually happen?

Your success in network marketing is going to be directly related to your roots. The first time that I heard that statement, I thought to myself, "It is hopeless then. My roots date back to a bunch of thieves, con artists, and hooligans in Ireland. How am I ever going to make it?" Orjan Saele, an incredible network marketing millionaire from Norway, and a personal mentor of mine, went on to tell the audience that he was not talking about your family tree. He was talking about the depth of your business. The secret to creating a lifetime residual income is building depth properly and tap rooting. Before anyone could ask him what tap rooting was, he began to tell the story of the Chinese bamboo tree. Chinese bamboo trees are grown all over Asia.

How this tree grows creates the ultimate parallel to building your network marketing business. Farmers plant thousands of bamboo seeds throughout acres of fertilized soil. Within weeks of planting the seeds, the farmers see a tiny little shoot break through the ground. The farmers are careful not to disturb this little shoot as they continue to tend to the soil, ensuring that the bamboo tree has the best growing environment. A year later, nothing has changed. The farmer has toiled in the fields every single day, watering the trees during times of drought and protecting them from rain. The farmer remains vigilant to ensure that the sprouts are not touched. Two years later, the farmer continues to work on the fields, but doesn't see a thing change. After four years of constantly working on the fields full time, ensuring that the optimal growing environment has always been there, the farmer still see no change. How many farmers could keep working on the same field for four years without any return on investment (ROI)?

In the fifth year, the Chinese bamboo tree starts to grow, and rapidly! In the fifth year, the tree grows by over three feet a day until it is ninety feet high. Why did do the trees wait for five years to grow? What is happening all that time? In the first five years the bamboo tree grows one massive root straight down, a tap root. In order to handle the weight and stress of that major growth spurt, the tree must prepare itself with a strong center, root deep into the ground.

You need to build a tap root in your own business

Tap rooting is the art of building deep into your business. Learning the art of tap rooting properly will ensure that you create real duplication in your business, and that you have a business that you can walk away from. Tap rooting starts when you're an apprentice by learning to get started properly. Understanding *The Most Important Minute* strategies, and using them, is the first step to learning tap rooting. Tap rooting is the art of teaching others how to get started properly, the art of teaching others *The Most Important Minute* strategies.

As an apprentice, you will study all of the teachings in this book, and many other great books. As you get your license, so to speak, you will begin to practice the things you have learned, independently. As you progress, you will begin to introduce others to the things that you have learned.

We have already established that when you sign someone up they are at on emotional high. You need to "strike while the iron is hot" and get them engaged. The first meeting, making their list, reviewing the websites, and booking the first in-home meeting are all important parts of getting someone started.

Tap rooting is driving depth

Your goal is to help get as many people started as possible in the depths of your group. You are going at a great pace if you are personally helping someone get started in your group every week. We are not just talking about your personally sponsored partners. I mean helping anyone in the depth of your business get started. You are going at an amazing pace if you are helping someone get started in your team every day. Remember, leadership is not the directions you give, but the example you set. Your goal should be to teach someone new in your team The Most Important Minute strategies as often as possible.

Whenever I get a new apprentice started, I tell them that I am going to help them do their first five one-on-one meetings and their first in-home meeting. Don't forget that new person is an apprentice. They are now in the learning zone and it is crucial for you to show them what to do. As I get that person started, I always tell them I am going to personally get their first apprentice started with them. I will actually do the first meeting, help them to make the list, identify the first five, host the in-home meeting, etc. Now you may ask, "Why are you doing that? Isn't that the apprentice's job? After all, it is their new distributor."

The reason I do this is so that my new apprentice will see exactly what to do.

I explain to them (and you) that I will do this over and over again until the leg is twenty new people deep. Every time I do a new meeting, I encourage my apprentice to be there, but I don't put any pressure on that new apprentice to participate.

I know you think it doesn't make sense. How does anyone become independent with this type of behavior? It is the first thing I thought too when I was first taught to tap root. The idea is that as you are tap rooting and getting people started, you are telling everyone the strategy, and suggesting that when they feel they are ready to go out and tap root the other legs the same way . No one is going to get rich with one leg growing. The apprentice is going to have to start and tap root several other legs before their paycheck grows, and now they have seen exactly how to do that.

As you are tap rooting your business, stay focused on the objective. As you are tap rooting, the people you bring in are going to see what you are doing. By the time you are ten to twenty levels down, you are going to have two to three people who have naturally started to duplicate you. By the time you are twenty levels down in your tap root, you will never have to worry about that leg again. When you have identified a few leaders in that leg, go on and start another tap root in another of your legs. Just like the Chinese bamboo tree, when your tap root becomes strong and secure, your income will soar!

Chapter 12: Become a Mentor

"When the student is ready the teacher appears."
Unknown

So now you know the secret! By understanding what the most important minute is, and how to use it, you now have the best chance at creating a profitable business within your team.

The network marketing business is really one of the simplest businesses on the planet. As an example, compare it to a McDonald's franchise business. To open a McDonald's, it will cost you millions of dollars in cash and thousands of hours in time. To start a business in network marketing, it will cost you hundreds of dollars in cash and thousands of hours in time. It takes the same amount of time and effort to open and build a franchise business, but the return on investment is much higher in network marketing.

To learn more about this side-by-side comparison, and why network marketing is the ultimate home-based business, purchase my book, *Next Century Wealth*. To succeed in the business all you have to do is learn two simple skills: business-specific leadership skills, and how to talk to people better and more. Once you learn these two skills, then the last part is to teach these two simple skills. That is the entire business. You didn't have to pay $2000 for that business plan.

Before your income is $10,000 per month, you will already be mentoring other people. In fact, that plateau is usually when your mentoring skills have to be honed. Network marketing is likely the only profession that you actually have to do before you can teach it. The entire business model is based on experience. You will not need to mentor anyone until you are well on your way to 10,000 hours, although you will start teaching the business much sooner than that. If I were going to quantify it for you, I suggest your teaching the business to others phase will begin around 1000 hours, but it will be different for everyone.

So who do you mentor?

The last thing you need to worry about is who to teach. Be patient. When you are ready, there will be more students than you could ever handle.

Early on in my network marketing career, I used to run around giving advice. It was bad. I ended up offending people regularly. I didn't realize that most people who join the business join because of the product and the paycheck, but they stay because of the community. The people in the business become their friends, their family, so they end up finding more value in the people. I didn't get that until Art Jonak, an amazing MLM rock star, leadership teacher, and friend, taught me that. Art has poured hundreds of hours into me and taught me one of the most important lessons of all: our business is about accepting people where they are at and loving them.

Be a mentor to those that come along asking.

You are going to be tempted to offer help throughout your career, to push people, but if they're not asking, then don't be pushing. You will know exactly who to spend your time with when the time comes. Spend your time with the performers in your team. If you ensure that your upline teams provide for you, everyone gets plugged into the training system and recommend them to read *The Most Important Minute* then you have fulfilled your obligation to them. After you get them started right, give them room to perform. When people in your team start to perform, you will know because they will start to advance in rank, win contests, and earn income. It is then that you begin to coach and mentor. But understand this very important rule about mentorship:

> *First there is relationship*
> *Then there is friendship*
> *Then there is Mentorship*

People will not take advice from you until they know you and trust you. They have to believe in their heart that you truly care about then. You will be ineffective mentoring anyone in your team before you build a friendship with them. So follow these steps to identify the right people to spend your time with and mentor.

Step 1: Identify the potential student through their performance.

Step 2: Watch your student to ensure that performance is real.

Step 3: Build a friendship with the person over at least thirty days.

Step 4: Continue to work on friendship and let them see you building the business and personally recruiting new people.

Step 5: Wait until they ask for your guidance.

In my book, *Being the Change,* I spend a great deal of time talking about mentorship. The world's greatest leaders and success stories attribute a major part of their success to their mentors. In the book, we talk about how to identify that you need a mentor, how to set up the mentoring relationship properly, and how to determine if a particular mentor is right for you. I strongly encourage you to go through that chapter.

If you are an apprentice or a prospect, then find a good mentor to help you with the shortest path to your success. The perfect mentor will be someone in your upline or support team as they will benefit financially from making sure you are on the right path. All of the energy and passion in the world will not replace the experience of a good mentor!

Chapter 13: It Is Up To You!

"Ability is what you're capable of doing. Motivation
determines what you do. Attitude determines
how well you do it."
Raymond Chandler

Okay, so you figured it out! The most important
minute is not really a minute at all. The strategies we
have talked about in this book will guide you through
your entire journey in our profession. As we close
out our time together here, it is important for us
to agree that commissions are generated when
products/service are purchased by customers and
distributors; anything other than that is illegal. So to
that end, the secret to success in network marketing
is to never stop looking for prospects.

Governments around the world are constantly reporting that things are getting worse. Economies are flat, at best. As long as governments continue to turn a blind eye to the need to true leadership education in the public school systems, there will be a huge need for what we offer: *freedom*! People are joining our profession at record numbers because it is seen as the last bastion.

Although it is sometimes possible to identify a great candidate at first glance, and maybe figure out a few more after a brief conversation, it is impossible to know definitively who will and who won't. Your best course of action is to decide to introduce people to your business opportunity every day.

If you were to introduce the business to just two people per week, by that I mean sit down with a prospect with your presentation kit and product samples, and go through the plan. Then you would be sure to sponsor one new prospect per month (with the proper follow-up, of course). That would give you twelve new apprentices a year. Using *The Most Important Minute* strategies for getting your apprentice started right, and tap rooting, you could surely turn those twelve apprentices into a team of hundreds of people. I wish I would have been started properly in the business. I wish someone would have recognized me as an apprentice, and taught me *The Most Important Minute* strategies.

It wasn't until I attended the MLM Mastermind event in Houston, Texas, in 2005 that my eyes were opened up and I started to learn the strategies that I have set out in this book. Thank you, Art Jonak, for your dedication to our profession!

It wasn't until I started reading *Networking Times Journal* that I truly began to understand the secrets to creating true generational wealth. Thank you, Chris and Josephine Gross, for your dedication!

It wasn't until I started reading an hour a day, started focusing primarily on growing myself, until I realized the power of PDCA (plan, do, check, and adjust), until I started listening to high quality leadership audio recordings for an hour a day, until I realized that I needed to be a better leader—it wasn't until all of this happened that God revealed the true abundances of life to me. Thank you, God, and the millions of network marketing professionals that walked before me. I firmly believe you will have a much easier time in the business if you get started properly. The practice of network marketing is a lifetime journey.

Creating habits of success

It has been proven time and time again that it will take you twenty-one days to truly create a habit. If you want to start going to the gym daily, you have to remember to go every day for the first twenty-one. If you are trying to remember to get on your morning Taking Action call every day, set your phone alarm every day for the next three weeks. If you want to get in the habit of telling a loved one how much you care every day, remind yourself for the first three weeks.

I know this sounds simple and too good to be true. Try it and see for yourself. I felt like someone had unlocked the door to success when I first heard this. I started applying the twenty-one-day rule to everything I was trying to set as habit in my life, and it worked. I got in better shape, I started reading more, I started listening more. To capture the full awesome power of *The Most Important Minute* strategies, grab the individual pieces and create habits.

As you start to make *The Most Important Minute* strategies part of your business and life, you will be amazed at the growth in your business. You can't grow your business until you start to grow yourself.

The law of numbers

The secret is that there are no secrets. Building a successful network marketing business is a numbers game. If you want ten to twenty new apprentices a year, you have to show the plan to 100 to 200 new prospects per year. One of the biggest problems in our business is not getting people to join; it's getting people started once they join. You can't change the numbers, so when you finally get your first apprentice started, it is crucial to get them started immediately. Remember where your new apprentice is emotionally and how soon that emotion starts to fall. The window is very small. Don't miss it.

If you are already in and are realizing that you were not started properly, and you understand how it has slowed your progress, don't worry, you can start again. I did. I joined the profession in November 2003. I didn't really start to understand *The Most Important Minute* strategies until after I met Art Jonak and attended my first MLM Mastermind in 2005. Everything you have read in this book I have learned since.

Another good friend of mine, and a business leader I regularly take advice from and follow his teachings, Orrin Woodward once said, *"Ken Dunn may well be the greatest PDCA artist I have ever met!"* Orrin is one of the top leadership gurus in the world today, and has been voted as one of the internet's top leadership bloggers. He is a co-author (with his best friend and business partner, Chris Brady) of the *New York Times* best-selling book, *Launching a Leadership Revolution*. Orrin has implied on several occasions that your success in any endeavor is closely related to your ability to make a plan, take action, review the action you have taken, and make adjustments when you see you are not getting the desired result. It was a great compliment when Orrin recognized my focus on intentionally tracking my progress and constantly making course corrections.

In his book *Flight Plan*, Brian Tracy likens the journey of a commercial airplane to the journey of life. When a plane takes off, it is off course 95 percent of the time it is in the air. Modern day aircraft utilize sophisticated computers and satellite navigations system to constantly adjust the directions, and do it so precisely that the computers calculate to the minute the time of landing, even on trips that are hours long. Tracy proves in the book that even though you don't have a GPS in your head, you can, and must, make those same corrections regularly when you realize you are off track. PDCA! When I realized that I didn't understand *The Most Important Minute* strategies, I quickly changed my entire business-building strategies and started from scratch. You can too!

Don't keep these strategies to yourself

The size of your group and income will be proportional to the amount of people you share *The Most Important Minute* strategies with. If you put a copy of this book in every teammates' hands, you will be giving them a great chance to understand what you now know. *The Most Important Minute* strategies are useless to you unless you apply them to your business and your life, and take action.

God has designed us all the same. We all have a heart, a mind, and an ability to move. We all have dreams, desires, goals, and passions. Make a decision today to take action. Use these strategies and be the change you wish to see.

NOTES

NOTES

NOTES

NOTES

Ken is one of the leadership training world's up and coming great speakers and trainings. An incredible hunger to learn and teach others has lead Ken successfully through five different professional careers in the past 25 years.

Ken began a policing career at the age of 18. He was involved in the policing world's most exhilarating and challenging disciplines, including undercover drug and surveillance work, S.W.A.T team work, aggravated child abuse, frauds aggravated assaults, illegal weapons smuggling, and homicides.

The birth of Ken's first child left him yearning for a career change. In the next ten years, Ken opened four different home businesses in four different industries (importing, property management, mortgage, and direct sales) and made millions of dollars from home in each profession.

In direct sales, Ken has assisted in building communities in excess of 250,000 people in over forty countries. Ken has helped dozens of families create new lives for themselves and significant seven figure incomes. As well, Ken has consulted with several direct sales company owners to successfully launch and scale their businesses around the world.

In 2008, Ken published his first book, *From Here to Having It All*, which attracted significant attention and sold thousands of copies. Ken has also published a number of popular audio and video training sets, which are now commonly used as reference tools in the direct sales and mortgage industries. Ken is a living example that a sharp focus on leadership development and relationship building will yield success in any endeavor.

Today, Ken regularly speaks to groups in the |direct sales, mortgage, insurance, and banking industries. He uses humor and his own experiences to inspire audiences around the world.

Ken lives in Toronto, Canada with his wife Julie, and children Matthew and Laura.

www.facebook.com/kendunnleadership

Publishing and Ordering Information

The Most Important Minute In Your Network Marketing Career

by KEN DUNN

Available online at:
www.evolvlifepublishing.com
www.amazon.com

For more information about bulk purchasing,
or affiliate marketing sales contact
EvolvLife Publishing directly
at: 1 (416) 477-1219
or info@evolvlifepublishing.com.

EvolvLife Publishing
1305 Morningside Drive, Unit 15
Scarborough, Ontario, Canada

www.kendunnleadership.com

Check in with Ken regularly and read his latest entries on leadership and life. Ken has developed a reputation globally for his tenacious study of all things leadership. He believes that all success in life starts with developing an ability to lead. The blog chronicles his studies, with a sharp focus on leading one's self. If you have ever had a true desire to become a better leader, start here!